THE RED BOWL

THE RED
BOWL

a fable in poems

Holaday Mason

Red Hen Press | Pasadena, CA

Book design and layout by Nicole Younce

Library of Congress Cataloging-in-Publication Data

Names: Mason, Holaday, author.
Title: The Red Bowl / Holaday Mason.
Description: First edition. | Pasadena, CA : Red Hen Press, [2016]
Identifiers: LCCN 2015050377 | ISBN 9781597097277 (paperback)
Subjects: | BISAC: POETRY / General.
Classification: LCC PS3613.A8167 A6 2016 | DDC 811/.6—dc23
LC record available at http://lccn.loc.gov/2015050377

The National Endowment for the Arts, the Los Angeles County Arts Commission,
the Los Angeles Department of Cultural Affairs, the Dwight Stuart Youth Fund, the
Pasadena Arts & Culture Commission and the City of Pasadena Cultural Affairs
Division, the Ahmanson Foundation, and Sony Pictures Entertainment partially support
Red Hen Press.

First Edition
Published by Red Hen Press
www.redhen.org

For Reid Stuart Mason
4/22/1956 to 9/14/2012

For Jack, who left when I was six months old and never came back.
And for Reid, who had Jack's eyes.

Contents

The Red Bowl

"Man has no body distinct from his soul, for that which is called the body is that portion of the soul discerned by the five senses, the chief inlets of the soul in this age."

—William Blake
The Marriage of Heaven and Hell

"When I love you, your breasts shake off their shame."

—Author unknown

THE CAST OF THE RED BOWL:

Scarletta *wed* The General _____ unknown woman
born & died/   born & died   born & ?

      +   +

Rosalinda *wed* José   Diablo
born & alive   born & alive   born & alive

   +
The dead

1. *Jesus*	*born & died in September*
2. *Deirdre*	*born & died in October*
3. *John*	*born & died in November*
4. *Two*	*born & died in December*
5. *Spilled Time*	*born & died in January*
6. *La Luz*	*born & died in February*

The Hours
Jesus, the First Tarantula
The Seven-legged Tarantula
The Original Swallow
The Silver Hummingbird

The Wolves
The Baseball Diamond
The Moon
The Town (The Goats)

ROSALINDA'S SECRET

If his chin were cleft
she would name him John,
and hoped for this
because it caused in her
a kind of feeling
recalling the possibility of life,
not death, but *esperanza,*
as her mother would have called it—
the necessity for each human
to follow a specific song
coming from the future,
not yet really heard,
but calling, nonetheless,
and with some variety of cadence,
so leading each to the place
of their destiny, the result
of which comprised
the basket of their pleasure,
full or spare, depending
on either a tin or well-tuned ear.

And if one had natural gifts—
enormous breasts, for example,
or legs like a colt,
a nose sharp for the body's oily desire,
the talent to sauté the tails of pigs
to crispy delicate morsels,
or an abundance of hair—red,
curled of course, as her mother,
Scarletta's had been—

a woman who'd said loudly, often
that women were at the height
of their beauty
when they turned forty-five,
an age after which she'd refused
wearing colors other than purple
or purplish blue, sometimes
turquoise with flares of green,
her body leading always
with the most magnificent face
the town had ever seen or any town
within the circumference of their myths,
which went back a hundred years,
so long in fact that she herself,
after death, would become
no longer simply a woman of strength,
but a tale from the Mexican desert—
the redhead whose beauty
had caused yellow iris to bloom
year after year near the spring
in the hills behind her latrine.

If his chin were cleft
Rosalinda could hope for José's
kiss again, imagining her own mouth
tasting like the sweet warm mangoes
that sometimes fell
from the trucks weaving
through the flat, forbidding desert,
lifting monuments of dust

that inevitably settled
all over her fresh harvest
of morning eggs, line-drying clothes,
dust that saturated
the western sky with ribbons
as ruby as the iridescent red plate
her mother had kept at her bedside,
that red bowl that had bounced
out of just such a delivery truck,
rolling lopsided yet unbroken
to the gate of the pig pen,
in a rattling sphere of forbidden
sexual color.

If this new baby's chin were cleft
his name would be John,
he would carry Scarletta's
gift for hope in his loins—
the desire of a lion,
yes, if the child had this fire
he might do more than survive,
since it was the only gift perhaps,
that might carry one to look
beyond the weevils in the grain,
beyond the asshole of the pig
sashaying past, even after being
hand-fed.

SCARLETTA SINGS INTO THE CLOUDS

There are specifics.

You must find them.

The General could hear

the blood, the quivering

music in my chest.

I, in turn, saw his shell-

shaped heart perfectly—

that pastel scalloped brother

of lung where all begins

and all, then ends.

If you follow

to the very edges

of love—

there, a knife can't stop

the song of a babe

or a wolf—

the song of an opal . . .

There are people

who belong to us.

The First Red Bowl

The women in town had bodies
stiffened like loaves of stale bread.

They carried their mother's
soiled laundry up hills, drank old goat's milk

and prayed into the narrowest pan,
cooking nothing but sand and then not even.

Rosalinda was born gleaming in cool pearled blues.

Wild horses came up the road,
kicked gravel onto the porch

as if smelling fresh water.
Scarletta's cunt was a valley of blood.

The red bowl near her right hand
and its meticulously kept objects were splattered.

But, in the warm wet red sheets,

the babe radiated those blues, those light greenish yellows.

In the second hour, she opened her eyes,

stared right through her mother to what lay beyond the door.
At the close of the fourth day,

her heart found a steady beat—

always slow,
slow as water transforming to air, to ice,

to rain, to soil.

Scarletta had never once felt
her child kick inside her womb.

On His Deathbed, the General Mariachi Recalls His Youth

When the tourist women wandered
at night, they'd give us money to play
while we, in our black suits and ruffled white blouses
hung around in the shadowy archways
of corridors surrounding the central park,
orange and hot pink carnation petals—
left behind from the peasant women's daily
stalls—sticking to our shoes.
We loved taking tourist money, watching
their white hands extend like beggars,
laughter whistling through our teeth,
plucking maybe one note or two on the big bass
guitar, perhaps a single E string descent
to tease them as we hugged our instruments
tight to hard thighs, rocking the rhythm
of the music against our groins, our chests,
talking, smoking, drinking, but never laying
those rhythms out into their full breath,
until the ladies shuffled off in shame,
our howls kissing their necks as they stumbled
down the narrow, cobbled streets of town.

The night when the truth came
was no different—proud in our black & white,
long hours after one, we lugged our instruments
on our shoulders in drunken zigzags
toward a white, white woman who waited
to snap our photo as we crooked around
the corner to the last open bar.
On film, she captured my shoulders,

my slim triangle hips, Mario's whore
curls, the tipped swaggers of our lips,
then disappeared like an ant in a hole.
She flew back to a state by the salted sea,
where that *wappa gringa* reproduced us in multiple
images small as daggers, cut out our silhouettes,
then hung our forms like a flock of caught crows
from a high ceiling under which she would lie
on a rich man's rug, chuckling and touching
herself until our bellies hurt so much sometimes
we couldn't make love to our wives,
who became suspicious.
From then on we were more careful.
And I began to see the seriousness of women.

THE FIRST TARANTULA, JESUS, SPEAKS TO THE EARTH

We do not ask what you are made of.

Not teeth, rotted flesh, ash, stone,
bone, lava, larvae, fish scales, coiled petals,
skulls, or wood. We do not think of you

as separate from our many legs—you're one

with this eighth note slide, loose sand and mineral
glint to the pools of water left in the secret folds of blue cactus
most mornings.

We know your eyelids never open.

We are your slightest sigh, furred and dark
and waiting for nothing since you are nothing
more than all of us conjoined.

Jesus, on the Mound of the Dead Babes, Raises His Front Legs

I am the strings of the first guitar—
its etched notes, the hushed step,
and then, dim again, halt
of me, all night as I write secrets
across the sand's constantly shifting pastel flesh.

The desert is a house of bones,
disintegration the hymn of dusk.

The sound of your soul, the one you left
in the pocket of an apron or soiled shirt,
this would resemble my heartbeat, the thrum

of which only the very calm and brave can fathom—

not the haunted wolf, nor the white stars,
with their lavish gazes of sadness, their desires.

These two are obvious, so I can say them plain—
the living, the helpless all crumble,
leaving small odd puzzles of decomposition,
reeking, glowing with temporal gore,
until even the memory of their hours
disappears
in the softest waltz,
like the fluted loft of a woman's turquoise skirt
*tumbling around her ankles in a fallen sky.**

Everything is born just once, no more.
For some, the heart's opening is equal

to the body's failure—a little ruin,
a bit more night and oh, the sorrows
of the living.

The Old Father, José, Addresses His Lost Child, La Luz

If I told you a wolf guards your grave
I'd be lying and telling the truth.

Because you get so cold at night,
this is my reason for standing at the ready—
it is always for love I have stayed the night.

And your mother stirs before every dawn,
finding me returned to the chair
near the window, never knowing I'd gone.

And your mother has lost five ribs
in her weeping.

They dissolved into
the bed sheets, staining the cotton
with the great blue wings of grief.

She recalls your wrists,
the ample lavender of your blood,
though you were absolutely new.

When she sleeps, I go to you
like a knife sliding between
day and night and wait

for the desert to begin dancing
as it will, privately, the granite boulders

rearing up as new stars
open their baskets of light,
the sky gathering bulk

around the hill where you lie
with the other babes in the graveyard
like a doll of bones.

But, I tell you, what is most
unusual is the ballet of the tarantulas—
quiet and skilled.

I am privileged.
Many have given me
their names and like black pearls,

I've had them tattooed
in the shape of a baseball
diamond across my back.

Even the youngest horses have grown
accustomed to the shadowy streams
of the tarantula's visits.

The entire town prays its piss prayers for us
in their withered strips of deadened words.

They stay far away
from the road because they've glimpsed
the odd fires of our lives
burning from these lands.

They look away,
tending to their corn, their infants.

As for the spiders, dear one,
I would never keep them in a jar,
even one blessed by the virgin's pink breath,

not knowing how you,
my lost soul,
my rib and song,

must stay coldly
inside the earth
after so little time spent

beyond the salt of your mother's womb—
and for this the tarantulas recommend me.

The Unrequited Love of the Seven-Legged Tarantula

It was obvious to all but me
(the bone children,
the wolves, the hours)
how badly I'd fallen in love
with the moon.

This was no recompense
for her (for she is a queen)
forced as she's been to run
her glint smooth fingers
along my ugly back, humble,
slung guttural hunk spider low, low
before her blistering eye of light,

the trance of which led me
farther, farther into the desert,
to José's gathering mounds—
that howling man who hates
guitar music—I limped to the place
he arrived every night.

Starting in autumn, each month
he dug up one little hillock,
then another, until there were six
dark pools
of disturbed dirt.

And as
the graves grew in number
I, a low spider,

grew more entranced
with the moon's cool face.
So did José.

We fell in love
because she is so full
of promise and luster—

the thick song of her desire
for freedom casting a glamorous spell
over what, in bleak daylight,
was a pitiful innocuous hill
in the otherwise faultless
flatness of northern Mexico.

ROSALINDA IN THE DAWN

I am surprised
to find myself happy

when I crack fresh eggs into the yellow bowl

and sometimes when Diablo's
guitar music skips up our empty dirt road

and onto my shoulder like
a chirping bird plucking at my earrings

making my hips sway again,
and sometimes as I feel José slide into bed

beside me, his thighs and chest dead
cold as he drags night

from the sky, asking me silently
to bring him back to morning,

his body still coming to mine
under the worn blankets, still adoring

the fallen doves of my breasts.

Even after we have been
taught not to hope, we do.

He believes I don't know
of his wanderings.

I give him the power of his secret.

The General
Mariachi's Love

We are all virgins
before we're born—

untouched, therefore
so clean
we have no hurt.

We are not a color
yet, not a sound—
other than that of a long,
long distance
or maybe of soil.

Of your mouth
I remember everything,
Scarletta. The
presidential rose
of your lips remains
the last thing
in my mind
before death with
its stupidity,

its arsenic scent,
came, sucked
my skull dry. At
that very moment,
I remembered your
blossoming nipples
spreading under my mouth,

then the long awful canal
of my mother's body

before the first hot
expression of my self
coursed into the light,

which was, of course,
unmentionable.

NAMES

I was pregnant six times.
I lost, perhaps somehow, I murdered each one.

The ceilings of the rooms of the dead
have a specific color.

Guess the color.
It's the color of language.

They have none.
But I will give them names now.

La Luz was the last, yet stayed longest,
still stays with us both.

She'd have been a house painter
had she lived, shouldering ladders

and cans of pastel paint
up hilly crooked streets like a man—

doing, then doing again,
whatever necessary.

Deidre was made of pure hate,
a hungry ghost chewing holes

into the windowsills
of my nipples

with her hard greedy fear.
The only life for her would

have been as a widow, so it's
best she never lived,

knowing as she would have
only an endless emptiness.

John remained four days,
quietly fixed on the November moon.

He never whimpered even
when he grew blue, blue,

and came back as the cat
who every morning licked

my ankles and later licked up
all of the splatters of my heart's blood.

Jesus of the seven fingers
had a superb umbilicus which swept

the floor when he flushed from
my womb. He moved slowly

as if made of precious oil.
This babe, Jesus, was entirely

of José, which now, in retrospect,
seems what drove my husband

to talk to boulders and tarantulas,
to keep company with wolves.

There was the hint of a girl-child
called "Two" although she was really

the fifth we made and lost and after
her there was another who gave me

visions of clouds. I named that last one,
"Spilled Time." When *she* left,

Scarletta's dormant golden iris burst
up, then down my hillside like ribbons of fire

while Diablo came to stand day after day,
often a quarter mile from the house,

pointing his chin to first sky, then earth,
scanning with his saw-blade eyes

as if counting stars,
or surveying each new thrusting flower.

When there seemed to him to be enough
blooms, he began tuning his coal black guitar.

José Considers the Baseball Diamond He Has Built in the Desert

Humans make no sense.
They make symbols,
theories maps and machines,
while ten thousand worlds
revolve within each blade
of grass, each ant.

The baseball diamond
in the village is both circular
and square, scuffed by feet
at four bases, the corners
of a perimeter men
themselves have conjured.
Reality otherwise overwhelms.

There is fire/earth/air/water
all around us and seemingly constant—
then, the outfield named as such for
obvious reasons.

But there were six of you
coming to Rosalinda's womb
as you did for six months—
half a year—filling each
month with first presence,
then absence, like the passage
of the minutes themselves.

If we had known of God's intent
We'd likely have turned our
backs to each other in our bed—
my wife and I,

her hip length braids
now hanging like dried umbilical
amulets over our doors,
smelling badly of mold,
inviting all manner
of raggedy crows to sit along
the crest of our roof
and hawk their yellow bulls-
eye gazes at us.

I suppose to be sane
we must understand
our hatred well.

SIN

Deirdre was acid
at the back of my throat

the moment José
entered me and drove,

no, laid himself hard
again and again

into the deep depression
of my cervix.

Deirdre—the mouth—
the endless cry,

the want—
desire, restlessly grasping,

puking, then grabbing and feeding,
then sucking, then kicking,

until nothing was good,
was left and still, again,

she squeezed,
until hopeless,

hopeless,
until I called her fetal heart

the bleak well,
walking all night,

holding the scalding moon
in both hands,

like a moon that will not set,
or a sun that will not set.

And I was so, so afraid.

The Silver Hummingbird's Small Song: Vision

If a man's been in a war
and everyone dies but him

he might make his bed slim as a casket,
shove it near a wall.

If ever again he asks a woman to lie beside
him, he'll never touch her.

He might hear things after a certain hour,
then become one of those lost hours,

as he sees her beautiful collarbones
float away like birds.

ROSALINDA: THE FALTERING SOIL

Amazing how the golden fists
of nearly unclenched iris appear
just after the spears of rain
and grow around the edges of my house
like a fence of citron fire.

Look there, my little angels
at the devil's wet feral coils,
all those aching petals,
closed tight as an infant's eyes
or the throat before
that first long scroll of breath,
that staggered scream.

They bloom and bloom
as if to mock me—
all winter, before the long
months of sun arrive
and burn our own shadows
from dark corner—the blooming
comes and keeps coming
until I have no teeth
to chew my sorrow
or my breakfast.

Diablo Considers the Eyes of Goats

Despite his huge size, my father,
the General's mind was really quite quiet.
Few ever got close enough to hear
this startling absence of clamor, because his presence
set them off, bile nibbling at the edges
of their little minds—those townsfolk
who, furtive, but curious as goats,
sniffed and sniffed, then closed tight
against what they could never bear or comprehend.

Their gossip circled around his body
the same way the wild goats bunged up
the garden square every night,
clanking their way through
tipped over trashcans, scavenging
scraps of meat and moldy bread,
crushed carnations and candy wrappers,
trampling the planted beds of pansies.

The whole town nearly wore itself out
telling impotent tales—
rumor, hearsay, ripe snips
like the very tough old beef they ate—
lies told and re-told until
a lie seemed a truth, until
each person seemed to be
the story of a person constructed
from a story.

But finding a prize of garbage
does not make a goat a man.
And belief does not make a lie the truth
unless you believe it yourself
then act to make it true.

My opinion? It was
the over-large square of his shoulders.
It was the flaming music,
which he passed on to me—Diablo.
And, of course, they all had a greed
for Scarletta's juicy love—
even the women.
Perhaps, that tilt too, how his short right leg
caused a slight syncopation,
a swivel as he paced
the silvery garden after every evening thunderstorm,
setting the beat as flocks of doves
dove from the cathedrals,
the corridors and bell towers to swish and glide.

He ignored the red glares that followed him,
as they all watched, peeking
from their curtained windows
crooked doorways, always ready,
always hungry, always hungry.
And the man smelled of deep water,
cold, deep, water, especially
when he was walking—

THE ORIGINAL SWALLOW'S
SMALL SONG: THE DANCE

When a woman rises daily

in her own dark country,

she dreams, therefore it rains.

Sorrow causes longing.

Longing causes envy,
then more sorrow.

Envy carries damage
and damage brings

more sorrow, maybe lies,
most often, both.

Strange how the sky breaks

itself into tiny diamond pieces.

The heart, the heart

is so awfully, awfully

utterly, utterly human.

SCARLETTA SPEAKS TO DIABLO
AFTER THE FACT

You know, there were always flies leaping
around the tip of your father's nose,
and his words too, black leopard.

This desert is, like any forest, filled with jewels,
raked by wind and look, my precious
fool, how the moonlit flowers
resemble Rosa's shoulder blades,
the flutes of them fitting
exactly the size of your hands,
as your father's did my own.

She does not love you,
not as I loved The General—
nor can she, you being her sibling—
each my beloved's precious child.
Still, she needs your bloodline music
like the wolves need the kill, like wind
requires rain to calm its croon.

Seriously, Diablo, I'm alarmed now
at the increased lavender shroud around her.
Have you noticed how it wrinkles,
whistling when she moves,

it murmurs, naming the dead
over and again in long whispers
louder than any bright jay
or hunting hawk's screams.

My own voice I hear,
in its paisley entrails, calling,
of course, to my love—
Go to her. Undo the knots of her
sorrow with the spell of your guitar.

Let it sing her wilderness alive,
let her smell the oil
of your hips while she boils
you coffee then perhaps begins to speak—

But please never forget
José, his sweetness soured
with anger like the best cream to curd.

Go while he curls on the graves of the whisperers.
Go as he enters the tribe of The Hours.
Watch the sky for raggedy birds and
remember, always, the great ruby bowl of dust.

Go while Rosalinda's skin is still
parchment on which your father and I
can write our songs into your music,
go and give the message of life—
before it's too late and the sky burns
and the birds fall with cruel rain,
before the valley is returned
to its rightful owners—the tarantulas,
who have waited so long,
far too long, to go back to their dance.

The Web of Light

The shadow
of the swallow
crossed her back
as she hoed
the stone garden,
after the swallow
had stolen the hummingbird's
song, sharp as polished steel,
& lodged it in Rosalinda's womb.
At that moment, she knew
beauty was the sole match
for grief, the two passing
through one another again
and again like bride's white mantel
and her black shroud.

Oh, that lost original swallow,
who, in grim panic, flew
back & forth across Rosa's shoulders,
close enough to steal
ten silky hairs from each temple
and forever mark her
with the bruised lament
of all vanished nests, all cries
for ruined eggs and lost ancient
trees with limbs strong enough
to hold and bear, the way
Rosalinda's own empty womb
still held trickles of menses
that sometimes flushed

her thighs without warning
after quiet months,
dry as the river bed.

The dead were dead
yet strangely alive—
their gossamer cables,
swirling in pure electrical
currents, muted auroras, polished
webs swinging through the daylight
air, restless, yet certain, coating the hours
with a kind of liquid grace.

And yet she could tell no one at all,
since José, now near mad, was the
solo witness that she, a woman
soon old, had created six babes
in one year, losing them all
like an awful clock
wound, then unwound,
yet still ticking, ticking.

The truth? The unwitting swallow
killed the pure silver hummer
who'd tended the iris.
The truth? The error was forgiven
the moment it came.
The truth? Mistakes by their name
are always witless, fumbled—
yet done and redone. The truth?

Ask the one who numbered the days,
and then ask each day
the meaning of numbers.

THE DANCE OF SPILLED TIME
AGAINST ROSALINDA'S THIGHS

Listening from my garden
I knew I had to
enter what he played so well.

What touched my neck is what caused
me to return his bow, deeply,
from the waist, from afar.

        Everyone I love has black eyes
        like my own, like
        the man in the hat.

Spilled Time had had red hair.
Of this I am sure.
The man's head was covered,
but the fur of his neck was clear.

He knelt in the road to tune
his guitar, carefully and slowly.
His hat was plagued with hummingbirds.

The hummingbirds sounded
like tin trumpets.
He played the dusty road into mist.

The devil played the farm.

THE GENERAL'S GHOST
RECALLS SCARLETTA'S BREATH
ON HIS COLLARBONES

Scarletta understood
the tarantula's dance.

When she was dying
they came

and, in numbers,
crawled

the wrinkled satin
of her breasts,

her arms—furred
black eight-legged

emissaries of my mouth,
leaving a trail of kisses

that were mine,
all mine.

They came, to give
comfort, silent

shadows settling along
her neck, they nuzzled

her cheeks like rain
then softly fell in love

with the warmth
of her flesh

even after
the damage air

itself had made of her,
pulling her

closer, closer
to the grave

where no one,
not even I,

would any longer be able to taste her.

The Original Swallow Swoops Past

hally opp la la
the trees are skeletons,

urinals for the feral town cats
feral town cats, what roams

and rustles, looking for
meaty murder—

we all do . . . do bite the born,
hinky on hind legs,

born is to kill,
to eat the moment before us

beneath us, devour God time
distraction, silly hoot,

the flesh of life what feeds us.
who feeds us life but flesh—

to live is to murder life
to murder for reign is death . . .

hally opp shush shush . . .
the people in the town

of the smallest thoughts . . . hiddy do . . .
the smallest thoughts

on top to rule slits the throat of life
and not for food, which is magnificent—

I sleep some nights above cats.
they are sleeping, so never know.

THE DUET OF THE LINGERING CLOUDS

S: I would not wish this on anyone.

TG: No?

S: Who are you to talk? After all, look at yourself,
where are your strong arms beloved?

TG: I know, I know, so thin, I'm near disappeared like the white flowers
off the mountains.

S: The one's on the altar when we wed, the ones that opened like . . .

TG: You! Oh, the hours of smelling your red hair!

S: Remember my specialty, my stone blue soup?

TG: And your furred tarantellas, so small yet SO patient!
How they would watch you stir. How thin I am Scarletta.

S: No, your son Diablo, now he is thin, but not nearly as dead as you, my dear.

TG: Ha, You should talk! Remember, your flesh was mine in the shadows of the
cathedral. You screamed.

S: Cold and nice. Stone and thigh.

TG: Oh, best not to remember. It's good the goats run wild all over that town.
I like that!

S: I like it too. Your mother cut hair from my corpse you know.

TG: Pitiful spite, she stuffed throw pillows with it, she . . .

S: Red nether hair too. Amazing, the patience of spiders—they will have their day.

TG: I've still no patience when it comes to you, would have fucked you on the altar . . .

S: They dressed the virgin in pink silk meringue, is that some sort of joke?

TG: You see that new coffin store near the square?

S: Good thing that they left us to leak into the soil, to leak . . .

TG: And grow back as blades of grass! I want to come back and enter . . .

S: He has your nose my love . . .

TG: I would have eaten you to smoke, lost my hands inside you, burned your hair like incense . . .

S: He will not stop.

TG: He should not stop.

S: I understand. He has your nose, but not your silence. In fact, the music will end it.

TG: It's a deep spell to break.

S: For the love of the moon. Grief smells of ash, of ash and linen, it reminds me of . . .

TG: The shape of your hips . . .

S: The shape of your big bass guitar . . .

TG: For a love like the moon . . .

TG: Her grief smells of ash, of linen. It reminds me . . .

S: Of you . . .

TG: Of you . . .

José in the Church of the Pink Virgin

You are cruel.
Why not admit it?

You made the seasons.
Each year, you end winter

with green, then heat passes
with the sweet yellowing of the apple tree's leaves.

From this, it seemed there'd be some order.
The rules of baseball have served better than you.

There is steadiness in rules,
in perfectly constructed squares and mounds.

I have more faith now in tarantulas,
in wolves and music, in the effects of goats.

You implied each loss would be followed by harvest.
But this, it's not the truth.

THE ONE WITH ONE LESS LEG WATCHES THE SKY

Crows are measly creatures
meanly assembling in groups

so thick they spread the color
of absence and attack, attack

anything threatening, bending their oily
raggedy necks over any and all things strange,

squabbling with worms, fire ants,
their gristly screaming beaks greased

with carrion scraped from the road
before the dying are yet fully dead.

One can die alive then die again
and never know it.

THE HOLY SUPPER

What I cannot control

I've taken and broken
like a weevil breaks the grain.

It was so easy to open her

ribs—

glaring parchment knives,
gates to the unbearable orchestra

of light and in the end silence grew
where the pulse of pleasure
used to be.

Grief can open you
like a blossom

or close you like concrete.

Grief might make you beautiful.

JESUS JUSTIFIED BY AN EASTERN WIND

I am every Jesus.

I am tenderness.

I require guts.

I watch both burials
and conceptions.

I was on the windowsill
and no one saw me.

I raised my face
and took the moon

and slipped inside the woman.

I have no real stake
in the matter, only curiosity,

luminosity.

I have time
and there is no time,
so I have plenty.

The Silver Hummingbird's Last Small Song: Turning over in Sleep

So sorry, dear darkness, can't undo
a loosened bitter wand—

what one does is done and it's been
said. How many letters to the dead?

How many wings in the air at every dawn?
I cannot fly and can't return.

But still, I can regret.

DIABLO

I have little to say
and am of little consequence.
That's why you see so little of me.
But picture my cock
as *you'd* want it to be.
If you are male, make it small
or—whatever.
If a woman, make it perfect
for your form only.
I had narrow shoulders, but resembled
The General (my father) only in my nose
and hips. The rest is a made-up thing.
Often they dress me in black but really
I always favored blue,
pale, powdery, any gesture of blue,
navy, indigo, anything really.
I never drank & I was good with
animals, my mother's wild cats especially.
Had Scarletta been my womb,
the fire would not have happened.
It's true I could play guitar so the bulbs
burst from the soil but that goes
with the cock thing.
I am the gesture of an architect who
needed an arch, a place for others
to hide in shadow, a place the sun
can gather, then slip out before
any gathering is seen.
Sometimes this is what a son is
for a father—at worst.

At best he becomes his own man.
I am a telephone pole who
may seem a man from a distance.
A mirage, a lick of wind against
the strings of a guitar—left outside, un-played.
Figure on it this way:
I am hers & theirs & as such
would be happy to be yours.
Play me, as she did in her mind.
I bow to the winds of fantasy.
As you wish.
As you like.
Anything you like.
Whatever.
I'm easy.

THE SEASONS ESCAPE THE DYING HUMMINGBIRD'S BEAK LIKE STEAM FROM A KETTLE

I hear the feet of the flowers.
They are the same as the feet of the dancers—
all roots resemble one another in the dark halls.
It is dense down here, but lovely.

You have questions. I can't answer any.
All roots resemble one another in the call of becoming.
It is dark down here, but lovely, violet.

Humans are made of wanting—
All moments are boats crossing softly as a breath's pliant bones—
exactly the same way a soul is variegated, transparently vulnerable—
exactly the same way a soul and flowers are.

Humans are musical instruments and
every song pours from them.
Babies are beautiful so we love them.
The world is beautiful so you will try to stay.

COMBUSTION

José caught fire on a Thursday in broad daylight
while running into town.

He knew at last the horses were skeletons
and the tarantulas were turning themselves into headstones—
understood perhaps it's what they'd always been,

heard each dead infant's name clarified in each
beat of his own mulish heart—
Deirdre, José, Jesus—Spilled Time, La Luz—

If first words are not spoken, they're forgotten,
simply eaten by the weather.

José had never spoken. Not of love, or hate,
sorrow, fear.
Now, the meat of *her* heart
on his tongue tasted of violets, of mango
and the sticky pirouettes of her body—in love, in death,

became a combined spell, the one he'd thought to escape
as she'd lain so still, bright-faced
under the press of his knife, watching like a sad mother,

while he'd cut her open—

as the sweeping notes of madness
struck his eardrums like pins.

And then, clouds rushed in, then, the scribbled out messages—
zigzag tumult, shivering lighting.

But the fact he'd made it to town when at last he burst—
that the flames leapt, purely joyful, released,

from weed to wall to silver cross, haystack, wagon,
then, of course, to the church bell tower,

beneath which he'd wed Rosalinda, under the sugar-spun,
plaster-cast gaze of a faded virgin—another martyr,
another woman whose body was used by love—

the fact he still had the good luck to rupture
so completely when he finally went to flame
so completely that he set the town to blazing,

could only be attributed to the feelings
the township harbored against all things holy and profane.

How they despised the unlimited art of the red sky
they'd all watched from behind shut blinds,

swirling over Rosalinda's house as she'd wept—
the plumes of saffron light flooding through
the glinting ribbons of Scarletta's hair,
as she made love to The General in the bald noon sun—

the flint sparking over Diablo's head as he played the moon
up from hiding, until everyone should have gladly sighed
back into the arms of midnights greatness.

The townspeople's whispering, their envious core—
so many bitter scores—
called José to come.

He obliged and blew up against the afternoon sky,
hissing a high whistle as he melted into the square,
blood boiling until his bones exploded and flew,

a keening sort of song tumbling
through the smoke in a satin packed chorus

like six perfectly tuned guitar strings
played by the hands of a master,

as the long braids of charred matter and air
became the ropes of his children's hair,

circling every house in slim curls
of billowing purple, like scars turned lava—

and every townsperson froze and stared
before abandoning all and running
into the desert like rabbits.

ROSALINDA'S DREAM OF
WHAT CAME LAST

You got your wish, love.

See the wolves river over the soot-coated
ruins of the town.

If one quiets, elusiveness dissolves.

The body fails. Weeping over this
stops nothing but the silence.

Yet even the wolves leave markings of flight.
Their hungers keep them hunting.

My breath was the language of sky.
Clouds and stars seem sky children.

Listening to the desert, it was full of small curving stones.
I remember touching the small valleys of my body.
Some were very dark and cool.

Love makes us remember.
But hate might call us back to love.

You stood exactly where all things must.
You decided. Nothing special, really—

we all do it every day—does one run
toward a thing or from it?

It's almost morning on the spinning earth.

The tarantulas will migrate soon.
How they must ache to go home.

Look, José. My black eyes are open.

That is true moonlight falling in the desert,
like ash over stone. I was real flesh.

My organs are the brightest blue
around your lips.

You did not ruin me with your fear—
both of our faces are still visible in bald light.

After all, desire keeps us alive.

The Kiss

When the horses reared and ran,
when the caskets in the store
broke open like cheap pianos and
the fruit vendors fell asleep mid-conversation,
toppling pineapples and papayas,

when the old ficus trees ringing the square
turned shiver-dead-blue as if wounded,
just before I reached the town,
she came and kissed me,
touched me long, sweet,
binding as the slow whistle
of the world's sorrow.

My love, my Rosalinda,
her hair a crown of cloud,
hers, now, the bird's eye view
of the valley below.
She made sure my face was turned toward
the truth, forced me to watch
as the mares, the stallions blew up,
one after another, she turned me
from murderer to
witness as their bodies painted
cobblestone streets in fuchsia meat,
the cathedral which they ran near,
stained pink as a saint's birth.

As the Original Swallow swooped
through the blasting flames,
her wings the sound of real happiness,
her song crackling from her beak
like cold water from a closed well,

Rosalinda kissed the deep hole
of my mouth,
called me José, José
then returned the unmarred bits
of my soul to her folds.

Some of us creatures are born too soft, but
a woman never forgets her love.

DATURA! DATURA!
THE GAME

This is how we passed time
waiting, waiting, waiting.

We learned to run when
the guitar heated up—
the devil in the music
opened all the poison flowers.

Only I could not move.
Because of the moon,
because those black bees
swarming from the jimson weed
blooms, clouded my view
of her, dressed her in black lace
so, uncertain, I froze.

To touch me was
to crack off my limbs
like that myth stuff of ice.
Oh, I be captured by desire,
oh, voluptuous song.

But the rest of them were free,
darted eight legs
through every strum
as the dead ones rose up
like spiraling flowers
yes, yes! The babes
heard the guitar.
Yes, yes, the babes

did rise, they did
and danced and danced,

streaming, hot as summer
open all through night
open to the night and hot.
They rose to the downbeat.
To the shush and sugar in one
river of one will—all six
and we go, we go too and quick.

José taught us.
Lift your hairy little legs.
Take the next base.
We all love to play baseball.

The Town after the Fire

Ghosts live three hundred years then begin to fade.
After El Fuego, the land became predominately blue.
Many times the soil was soaked
with waves of azure light & unusual movement.
Wilted stars collapsed over the roads,
in fact, decayed there like closed gates.

With a sharp eye, with strength, one could see
the dancing—no, really waltzing—
shapes of the men & women accepting
the night, hell & all that came after hell,
which was more a pond of tranquility,
a bath of their whispered passions
lingering between the hills, between
their old lives & the velvet sky,
which for them was devoid of planets.

Tender winds whisked between each coupling
of pure lucid bodiless bodies whose sole
task it was to bridge the air with words
of love, admissions of lies, acknowledgments,
remembrances of daily things,
all gratitude, all guilt now laid
on the altar of death the way a woman
might rest her head on her beloved's shoulder.

The hazy dancers wafted in the concave
place where the town had been,
each step, smoldering cerulean, teal,
lapis smudged with lavender,

all opal luminescence, ghost souls
gleaming like a rich man's best shoe
or the mist of an infant's first sigh.

To those with a heart too young
or fear too great to bear sorrow,
the ghosts simply became a field of peculiar clouds—
the valley, a bowl filled with hovering
blossoms, pale undulating roses, gardenias,
dogwood, late apple, tulle petals
opening, open & open,
the wind entirely dense with disturbing perfumes.

Diablo Becomes a Telephone Pole

I heard a man say something I can't repeat.
That's actually often true.
There's a lot of hissing & apology in life.

These recorded voices for the money
fool only the badly lonely. Nothing new.

But these tourists, man, are so loose
with their cards, spelling each digit through
the wires. Black on black—I am the thin man
in black now, my chest a hanger for crows—

I like crows. I like Jim Morrison too.
Heard a boy who saw him out at Venice beach—

I hear there's a boardwalk full of *Playboy* boobs,
snake men & surfers. I'd like to visit, but

I get to travel the world of wishes & of lies. Good thing
I like standing in silence. I was invisible anyhow,
except to her, & then only visible in her madness.

I like the desert. The sun comes as a familiar mouth
night after night to kiss my shoulders, my nipples & then
the dark before the moon who is no one's whore.

Every Sunday noon I watch teenage boys
shuffle up the road, checking out each other's asses,
spit brushing up their black hair, copping smokes.

I get calls all the time. I play every sort of music—Tejana,
Bach—& can see from here the valley where Rosalinda walked.

Every time the wind is from the east, it hints
of Scarletta's feral cats, their stains hitting every last arch
in the corridor around the garden,
hints of her actual perfume: persimmon & gold dust,
& sometimes The General plays the slow music.

I am wired for sound.
Whatever you want I can find.
You just have to know how to ask.
So ask. Please.

THE BROKEN MEAL

I loved my wife.

I ate her heart because
she gave it to me when I was starving,

and she was beautiful.

I was never hungry before the infants came.

I know she lied

about the youngest mariachi, half brother—
of us all, really—that Diablo.

He left a trail like the music of the wind.

And even when she begged,

her pleading was tuned to his guitar.

The pearls from his heart lay like eighth
notes across my doorstep, a sonorous climb.

Regardless of whether
he entered her flesh, he entered her nonetheless.

The music made her again.
His eyes made her beautiful again,

while I listened to the baseball game
in my mind, with nowhere to go.

How we love order
and hate it too.

There is no end to it now, this,
day in, night out and

I love her much better than death does.

José & Rosalinda

We've said nothing
of butterflies.
We could speak of them.

There are few here in Sonora,
just the simple white ones filling
the barns in spring.

Beloved.

Its seems easy to say,
as if what is done is forgotten.

Decisions are houses.
Once we wove
a home and flesh
between us.

There are many sorts of love.
Remember that box from France?

The butterflies are in it still.
You'd press your fingers
into their color,

smudge your eyelids purple
open your arms and dance,
stopping at the window
to breathe in the powder sky.
Their names were French.

The dirt beneath the world
they'd flown through
was still on their wings.

Go get whatever is left in the box.
Where? Is it where it once was?

Beneath our bed,
my love, of course.
There are no "of courses"

in this world. Yes, I know.
Of course I know I know that's true.
Of course it is, of course.

The Original Swallow Is Reframed as the Silver Hummingbird

I am becoming floral, becoming soil, returning
to the darkness, that shuttle of heartbeats
through the hours which is the sound
of one woman getting out of bed
because she is not done living yet.
It is the sound of everyone.
Keep a good record if you can.
The body is mean with the intention of survival—
that is only true of the body & not the true body.
I never forgot the opal rings around stars.
They were what I carried on my wings.

The Red Bowl

I can't tell the truth.
I want to, but
I don't know what it is.

I found José eating my heart.
His fingers were broken,
shoulders black from learning
the tarantulas songs—their broken priest.

I forgave his hunger,
his nose smashed from weeks of nights,

cock shriveled as any goat's,
ribs bruised from calling

for the wolves who sucked
the meat from the bones
of my babes.

You can't stop hunger.
And murder does not always kill love.

I can't find my way out of the questions.
What human can? So

I confess. I loved. I listened.
My belly lifted

and the graves on the hill collapsed.
My legs parted and

tiny ruby birds flew out
and circled and circled and gathered

into a great red bowl as bright as
a penumbral dawn

thunderstorm, hovering over the town—
birds with no sound, just blinding

flinty candles of light
tearing their wings apart, as

their force tore every locked
window open, waking the ugliest,

poorest, the very young, flashing
like the inferno of Scarletta's hair

when she danced, when she hummed
The Hours into the scallop shell heart of

The General, when she licked her own blood
from his cock and crowed.

I danced the fire alive. I danced into it, while

the desert clamored to such blooms—
jimson, cactus, orange poppies, white rose.

I did it. I did.
I did it. I did.

And I was so, so happy.
And the sky was a red bowl of wings.

The Original Swallow Sings Her Oldest Small Song: Lost Poem

Why wolves?
Why the drift?
Why the yellow moon?
Why solitude & not Two?
Why not all hearts alive?

It's all fiction.
Tell me a story.
I have, I did.
Tell me again.
He throws back his head.
And howls.

Acknowledgments

Thank you is too small a saying to hold the reality of what my community of friends & my colleagues have given. Nor can I name everyone here, so please know that everything & everyone I've ever known, with any depth, has given to the making of the work, as it is with life & art. But I must name a few—Dr. Erna Osterweil who is my psychoanalyst; my dear brother, Reid Mason; Barbara Urschel and Bill Urschel; The beloveds: David St. John, James Cushing, Celeste Goyer, Gail Wronsky, Katherine Williams, Holly Prado, Lilly Dale Reed, Sudie Shipman, Laura Amazzone, Christine Lopez, Alan Davis, River Mary Malcolm, Christine Downing, Judith Pacht, Veronica Golos, Robert Hass, Jeffrey Levine, Louise Mathias, CD Wright, Harry Northup, Chuck Rosenthal, Richard Garcia, Brendan Constantine, Cecilia Woloch, Lynne Thompson, Fred Dewey, Marci Vogel, Marsha de la O, Phil Taggart, and Friday Lubina; Red Hen Press, especially my point person, Selena Trager; the people at Beyond Baroque: Carlye Archibeque and Richard Modriano; The Monday Poets: Jim Natal, Jeanette Clough, Jan Wesley, Marianno Zaro, Paul Lieber, Dina Hardy, Marjorie Becker, and Brenda Yates; also, Ralph Angel, Anne Fisher Wirth, and last but never, ever least, Sarah Maclay.

BIOGRAPHICAL NOTE

Holaday Mason is author of *Dissolve* (New Rivers Press, 2011), *Towards the Forest* (New Rivers Press, 2007), *Interlude* (Far Star Fire Press, 2001), *Light Spilling from its Own Cup* (Inevitable Press, 1999), and is co-author of the forthcoming *The "She" Series: A Venice Correspondence.*